GOLF'S
MOST OUTRAGEOUS QUOTES

GOLF'S
MOST OUTRAGEOUS QUOTES
AN OFFICIAL BAD GOLFERS ASSOCIATION BOOK

by Bruce Nash and Allan Zullo with Bill Hartigan
ILLUSTRATED BY PAT OLIPHANT

ANDREWS and McMEEL
A Universal Press Syndicate Company
KANSAS CITY

Library of Congress Cataloging-in-Publication Data

Nash, Bruce M.
     Golf's most outrageous quotes : an official bad golfers association
book / Bruce Nash and Allan Zullo with Bill Hartigan
          p.   cm.
     ISBN: 0–8362–1789–6
     1. Golf—Quotations, maxims, etc. I. Zullo, Allan. II. Hartigan, Bill.
III. Title.
GV967.N375   1995
796.352—dc20   94–47069
                                                              CIP
Designed by Barrie Maguire

DEDICATION

To Charles Segars, a clutch performer whose name stands tall on the leader board of life.
　　—BRUCE NASH

To Allan Stark, who, like most of us, talks a much better game than he plays.
　　—ALLAN ZULLO

To my aunt and uncle, Vera and Harold Spinaci, who in the game of life are two of its greatest players.
　　—BILL HARTIGAN

TEEING OFF

No sport generates more outbursts of rage, passion, and hilarity than golf. The game—which makes millions of dollars for the par-birdie-par pro and brings joy and heartache to the slice-your-drive, cut-your-Titleist weekend hacker—inspires a range of language from hellfire epithets to silver-tongued eloquence.

On the course, you rant and rave at buried lies and plugged lies, bunkers and bogeys, chili dips and recurring yips. You curse at your own misfortune and chuckle at the errant ways of your playing partners. Between shots, you serve up zany excuses for why your ball didn't go exactly where you had planned. And you offer your partner crazy advice after his ball didn't go exactly where he had planned.

Eventually, you stagger off the course and arrive at the 19th hole where you relive your only decent shot of the day—a nifty chip-and-run for par —and lament the banana balls that cost you a bunch of Nassaus. And then you and your fellow linksmen regale each other with good-natured putdowns and comebacks.

Throughout the week at work, you prattle on and on about a sport that both seduces and infuriates. Unfortunately, like millions of others, you can talk about the game much better than you can play it.

If only you could make birdies with the ease that you make golf jokes; sink knee-knockers with the frequency that you deliver knee-slappers; land approach shots with the skill that you turn a witty phrase.

It is the nature of this royal and ancient game to spawn flashes of wit, wisecracks, and wordplay. As noted golf historian Herbert Warren Wind once said, "Golfers talk a lot, and they talk very well as a rule. Out on the privacy of the course, invigorated by the sweet air and the spring of the turf, a man opens up. He speaks his mind candidly on almost any subject. Things strike him humorously, including himself."

This book is a collection of the funniest, nuttiest, and most outrageous quotes in golf. It's designed to appeal to every golfer who has ever duck-hooked a drive, bunker-whiffed a sand wedge, or deep-sixed an approach shot. In other words, it's for members of the Bad Golfers Association, a decidedly unprofessional organization of golfers who slice, hook, hack, and generally louse up the golf courses of America under the motto "Bad But Proud." Should your love of the game far exceed your ability to play it, consider yourself a member in good standing of the BGA.

Included in this book are wry comments from duffers, writers, presidents, celebrities, elected officials, and others who, through their hopeless caliber of play, have become automatic members of the BGA. But not all the quotes are from bad golfers. Quite the contrary. Although pro golfers are strictly prohibited from entering the hallowed ground of the Bad Golfers Association, they have, on rare occasions, displayed the type of golf which the BGA condones. The problem is, the pros don't seem capable of playing that way often enough. However, they have proven more than capable in coming up with outrageous quotes.

Whether uttered by a pro or a hacker, rib-ticklers, one-liners, and quick quips most often are born out of a memorable, inglorious incident that unfolded on the tee, fairway, or green.

For instance, during a tournament in England, 1993 Masters winner Bernhard Langer played a shot from about 20 feet up in a tree where his errant drive had landed. After knocking the ball out of the tree, Langer was asked what club he had used. Replied Langer, "A *tree* iron, of course."

During the 1964 Bing Crosby National Pro-Am, Arnold Palmer hit his tee shot on the par-3 17th hole over the cliff behind the green, into shallow water in front of the 18th tee. Back then, the bay and its beaches were played as part of the course. While Palmer pondered his shot, TV reporter Jimmy Demaret told viewers, "If he takes the option of dropping behind the point where the ball rests, keeping in line with the pin, his nearest drop is Honolulu."

At the 1978 British Open at St. Andrews, Tommy Nakajima was putting for a birdie 3 on the 17th hole. Unfortunately, the ball trickled off the green and into the feared Road Bunker. It took him four swings to blast out of the sand and he wound up with a shocking nine. "I must live with the dishonor they now call 'The Sands of Nakajima,'" he ruefully said.

His disaster was almost overshadowed by Peter Jacobsen's nightmare on the same hole at the 1990 British Open. P.J. walked off with an embarrassing eight—and felt thankful that he hadn't topped Nakajima's horror. Said Jacobsen, "I was able to escape the humility of having the left rough forever named in my honor as 'The Beater of Peter' or 'The Wake of Jake.'"

Pro golfers don't hold a monopoly on humor. Some caddies can deliver a line better than they can read a green. Perhaps no bag-toter possessed as sharp a tongue as St. Andrews's legendary Lang Willie. The caddie, who dressed in a stovepipe hat and a swallowtail coat, loved to drink. One time, an indignant R&A member accused Willie to his face of being drunk on the course.

"Aye," said the caddie. "But I'll get sober. T'ain't nothin' ye can do aboot that gowff game of yours."

Most pros can't resist taking a good-natured jab at their amateur playing partners.

The first time that Frank Sinatra played golf with Arnold Palmer in Palm Springs, Ol' Blue Eyes spent more time in the rough than on the fairways. After the round, Sinatra asked the General, "What do you think of my game?"

"Not bad," replied Palmer. "But I still prefer golf."

During a pro-am, a woman came up to Senior PGA Tour player Bruce Crampton and introduced herself as his amateur partner. Knowing

Crampton's reputation for saying few words, she told him, "I need your help. A friend of mine bet me $10 that you wouldn't say five words to me all day. You will talk to me, won't you?"

"Sorry, lady," Crampton replied. "You lose."

■

The outrageous quotes chosen for this book reflect the very essence of golf—BGA-style, that is. For example, humorist Dave Barry comments on dorks on the course . . . writer Rex Lardner on bad lies (the kind you tell) . . . Jimmy Demaret on golf and sex . . . Fuzzy Zoeller on the importance of the 19th hole . . . Gary Player on choosing between his wife and his putter . . . Roberto DeVicenzo on signing the wrong scorecard . . . Tommy Bolt on where to throw your clubs in anger . . . and Lee Trevino on the need for scuba equipment on the course.

Above all else, the quotes in this book remind us what the Bad Golfers Association stands for: Golf is a game to enjoy and not to take so seriously that we forget to laugh at our own frustrations, foibles, and flubs.

ADVICE

"Under an assumed name."
> —DUTCH HARRISON to a pro-am hacker who asked
> how to play the next shot

"Lay off for three weeks and then quit for good."
> —SAM SNEAD to a pupil

"Your clubs."
> —JACKIE GLEASON, when asked by Toots Shor what to give
> the caddie after shooting 211

"All you have to do is hit the ball closer to the hole."
> —VALERIE HOGAN to her husband Ben on his putting

"What you have to do is shoot the lowest score."
> —BEN HOGAN to Nick Faldo

"He told me just to keep the ball low."
> —CHI CHI RODRIGUEZ, on putting advice from his caddie

APPEARANCE

"Nice clods, Stadler. Did you get those at a Buster Brown fire sale?"

—FUZZY ZOELLER, commenting on Craig Stadler's new golf shoes

"I like golf because you can be really terrible at it and still not look much dorkier than anybody else."

—DAVE BARRY, humorist

"The uglier a man's legs are, the better he plays golf. It's almost a law."

—H.G. WELLS, author

"George, you look perfect, . . . that beautiful knitted shirt, an alpaca sweater, those expensive slacks . . . you've got an alligator bag, the finest matched irons, and the best woods money can buy. It's a damned shame you have to spoil it all by playing golf."
    —LLOYD MANGRUM to comedian George Burns

AUGUSTA NATIONAL

"What's the property of Augusta National worth? God only knows. But they haven't consulted Him. He's not a member."
    —Real estate broker to columnist Dave Anderson

"Amen Corner looks like something that fell from heaven, but it plays like something straight out of hell."
    —GARY VAN SICKLE, golf writer

"Nothing funny ever happens at Augusta. Dogs don't bark and babies don't cry. They wouldn't dare."

    —FRANK CHIRKINIAN, CBS sports producer/director

"We don't want to get anybody killed. Of course, if we could pick which ones, it might be a different story."

    —HORD HARDIN, Augusta National Chairman, postponing play
      in the 1983 Masters because of lightning

"There is a saying around Georgia that the Augusta National Golf Club is the closest thing to heaven for a golfer—and it's just as hard to get into."

    —JOE GESHWILER, sportswriter

"If there's a golf course in heaven, I hope it's like Augusta National. I just don't want an early tee time."
　　—GARY PLAYER

BAD LIES

"I'll take a two-shot penalty, but I'll be damned if I'm going to play the ball where it lies."
　　—ELAINE JOHNSON, LPGA pro, after her shot hit a tree and caromed into her bra

"The difference between golf and government is that in golf you can't improve your lie."
　　—GEORGE DEUKMEJIAN, former governor of California

"Check the diaper; if it's wet you get relief from casual water."
— BOB MURPHY, after his playing partner's ball landed in a baby carriage

"Hey, is this room out of bounds?"
— ALEX KARRAS to a startled bystander, after hitting a golf ball through the plate glass window of the clubhouse at the Red Run Golf Club in Royal Oak, Michigan

"Golf is a game in which the ball lies poorly and the players well."
— ART ROSENBLUM, comedian

"One reward golf has given me, and I shall always be thankful for it, is introducing me to some of the world's most picturesque, tireless, and bald-faced liars."
— REX LARDNER, writer

"Isn't it fun to go out on the course and lie in the sun?"
— BOB HOPE

"Some lies are believable and some are not. The technique of lying and the timing of lies are at least as important as mastering the drive."
—REX LARDNER, writer

"Couldn't one of you have kicked it into a better lie?"
—DAVIS LOVE III, after hooking a ball into the crowd at the 1994 Las Vegas Invitational

BETTING

"The loudest sound you hear on the golf course is the guy jangling coins to distract the player he bet against."
—JIM MURRAY, sportswriter

"Never bet with anyone you meet on the first tee who has a deep suntan, a 1-iron in his bag, and squinty eyes."
—DAVE MARR, golf pro

"So if you visit Chicago, enjoy the many great courses, the Midwestern friendliness, and the city's other amenities. But if a stranger with a goofy swing wants to play for more than loose change, take a pass. It's a long walk back to your hotel in bare feet."

 —MIKE ROYKO, columnist, on golf-course hustlers in the Windy City

BLOOPERS

"Famous midsouth resorts include Pinehurst and Southern Pines, where it is said that there are more golf curses per square mile than anywhere else in the world."

 —Typo in a North Carolina tourism booklet

"Now on the pot, Johnny Tee."

 —Los Angeles Open announcer, screwing up the introduction to pro Johnny Pott in 1965

BUNKERS

"Double bogey, double bogey, double bogey."
>—Caddie HERMAN MITCHELL to Miller Barber, who wondered what was behind a dangerous bunker

"My dear, did you ever stop to think what a wonderful bunker you would make?"
>—WALTER HAGEN to a buxom opera diva

"Once when I'd been in a lot of bunkers, my caddie told me he was getting blisters from raking so much."
>—JOANNE CARNER, LPGA pro

CADDIES

"If each time a player and caddie split up was actually a divorce, most Tour players would have been 'married' more times than Zsa Zsa and Liz combined."
>—PETER JACOBSEN, PGA pro

10

"Real golfers, no matter what the provocation, never strike a caddie with the driver. The sand wedge is far more effective."
    —HUXTABLE PIPPEY, writer

"The Royal Hong Kong Club caddies hit the nail on the head; their term for golf—'Hittee ball, say damn.'"
    —DICK ANDERSON, writer

"If a caddie can help you, you don't know how to play golf."
    —DAN JENKINS, writer

"I was lying 10 and had a 35-foot putt. I whispered over my shoulder, 'How does this one break?' And my caddie said, 'Who cares?'"
    —JACK LEMMON, actor, recalling a putt at the Bing Crosby National Pro-Am

"Caddies are a breed of their own. If you shoot 66, they say, 'Man, we shot 66!' But go out and shoot 77, and they say 'Hell, he shot 77!'"
　　—LEE TREVINO

"Why ask me? You've asked me two times already and paid no attention to what I said. Pick your own club."
　　—Caddie to Dow Finsterwald, at the 1960 U.S. Open

CHAMPIONSHIP GOLF

"Golf is 60 or 70 contestants over 200 acres doing unpredictable things at improbable times. It's an 18-ring circus without a ringmaster."
　　—NICK SEITZ, writer

"Golf, especially championship golf, isn't supposed to be any fun, was never meant to be fair, and never will make any sense."
> —CHARLES PRICE, writer

"The rest of the field."
> —ROGER MALTBIE, when asked what he would have to shoot
> in order to win a tournament

CHEATING

"[President] Nixon could relate to the ordinary guy who plays. Hell, I even once caught him cheatin' a little bit— movin' the ball when he didn't think nobody could see him. All hackers do that."
> —SAM SNEAD

"I have a tip that can take five strokes off anyone's golf game. It's called an eraser."
  —ARNOLD PALMER

"You know the old rule. He who have fastest cart never have to play bad lie."
  —MICKEY MANTLE, baseball legend

CLUBS

"A professional will tell you the amount of flex you need in the shaft of your club. The more the flex, the more strength you will need to break the thing over your knee."
  —STEPHEN BAKER, author

COMPLAINTS

"Some players would complain if they had to play on Dolly Parton's bedspread."
— JIMMY DEMARET

"There are two things that guys on tour do not like: playing in the wind and me dating their sisters."
— GARY McCORD, TV analyst and part-time pro

COST

"Your financial cost [of playing golf] can best be figured out when you realize if you were to devote the same time and energy to business instead of golf, you would be a millionaire in approximately six weeks."
— BUDDY HACKETT, comedian

"An expensive way of playing marbles."
— G.K. CHESTERTON, British writer, on golf

COURSES

"A golf course is nothing but a poolroom moved outdoors."

> —FATHER FITZGIBBON, declining a golf invitation from colleague Father O'Malley in the movie *Going My Way*

"Did you know what my favorite course was in college? Cafeteria."

> —MAC O'GRADY, PGA pro

"This hole is 614 yards. You don't need a road map for this one, you need a passport."

> —JAY CRONLEY, golfer, on the 5th hole at Southern Hills Country Club, Tulsa

"Par is whatever I say it is. I've got one hole that's a par-23, and yesterday I damn-near birdied the sucker!"

> —WILLIE NELSON, on the personal golf course he had built

"Golf at the Broadmoor represents one of the most interesting patch jobs since Baron Frankenstein started picking up free samples at the local medical school."

—PETER ANDREWS, writer, describing Colorado's Broadmoor Resort golf course

"If we played a course like this every week, there wouldn't be anybody left at the end of the season. We'd all quit the game."

—MARK CALCAVECCHIA, after missing the cut at the 1991 U.S. Open at Medinah Country Club

COURSE DESIGN

"I think I'll go cold turkey in the end and build golf courses. I'll torture other people."

—DAVID FEHERTY, pro golfer, on how he plans to leave the game

"If you birdie the 18th, do you get a free game?"

　　—JOHN MAHAFFEY, PGA pro, questioning the ultramodern
　　　design of the TPC at Sawgrass

**"I saw a course you'd really like. On the first tee
you drop a ball over your left shoulder."**

　　—JIMMY DEMARET to course architect Robert Trent Jones

DREAMS

*"I once had a dream where I made 17 straight holes
in one and I lipped out my tee shot on the 18th hole.
I was so goddamned mad I couldn't sleep."*

　　—BEN HOGAN

**"I never really dreamed of making many putts.
Maybe that's why I haven't made many."**

　　—CALVIN PEETE, Senior PGA pro

DRIVING

"Well, that lot's full. Let's see if I can park this baby someplace else."

 —JOANNE CARNER, after whacking two drives into an
  adjoining parking lot

"If there's a faster way to turn a Jekyll into a Hyde than by handing a man the driver, we don't know of it."

 —LEW FISHMAN, chief technical editor, *Golf Digest*

"Seve Ballesteros drives into territory Daniel Boone couldn't find."

 —FUZZY ZOELLER

"There are nearly 60 golf courses in the Palm Springs area and former president Gerald R. Ford never knows which one he'll play until he hits his first drive."

 —BOB HOPE

"I just hitch up my girdle and let 'er fly."
> —BABE DIDRICKSON ZAHARIAS, three-time U.S. Women's Open
> champion, explaining her long tee shots

**"If I had cleared the trees and drove the green,
it would've been a great tee shot."**
> —SAM SNEAD

"Man, I can't even point *that far!"*
> —GAY BREWER, Senior PGA pro, after watching a long-distance
> blast by John Daly

DUFFERS

**"Walter Hagen once said that every golfer can expect to
have four bad shots in a round and when you do, just put
them out of your mind. This, of course, is hard to do when
you're not even off the first tee when you've had them."**
> —JIM MURRAY, sportswriter

"I played Civil War golf. I went out in 61 and came back in 65."
   —HENNY YOUNGMAN, comedian

"The safest place would be on the fairway."
   —JOE GARAGIOLA, former baseball player, on the best
      place to be during a celebrity golf tournament

*"You've just one problem. You stand too close to the ball—
after you've hit it."*
   —SAM SNEAD to a pupil

**"My best score ever is 103, but I've only been playing
15 years."**
   —ALEX KARRAS, former Detroit Lions football player-turned-actor

*It matters not the sacrifice
Which makes the duffer's wife so sore.
I am the captive of my slice
I am the servant of my score.*
   —GRANTLAND RICE, sportswriter

"The flags on the green ought to be at half-staff."
— AL MALATESTA, amateur golfer, on his game

"I was three over—one over a house, one over a patio, and one over a swimming pool."
— GEORGE BRETT, baseball star

ENEMIES

"The golfer has more enemies than any other athlete. He has 14 clubs in his bag, all of them different; 18 holes to play, all of them different every week; and all around him are sand, trees, grass, water, wind, and 143 other players. In addition, the game is 50 percent mental, so his biggest enemy is himself."
— DAN JENKINS, writer

"I guess there is nothing that will get your mind off everything like golf will. I have never been depressed enough to take up the game, but they say you can get so sore at yourself that you forget to hate your enemies."
    —WILL ROGERS, humorist

EXCUSES

"If you pick up a golfer and hold it close to your ear, like a conch shell, and listen, you will hear an alibi."
    —FRED BECK, author

FUN

"Most people seem to have fun here . . . even when they're lining up their fourth putt."

> —BANKS SMITH, chairman of the grounds committee at Oakmont Country Club

"Golf is more fun than walking naked in a strange place, but not much."

> —BUDDY HACKETT, comedian

"People who say golf is fun are probably the same people who rationalize the game by saying they play it for their health. What could be fun about a game in the entire history of which nobody has ever shot the score he thought he should have?"

> —CHARLES PRICE, writer

"Tell me honestly: Do you know anyone who truly likes to play golf? Oh, I suppose there are some people who derive pleasure from golf just as there are certain kinds of individuals who enjoy being snapped in the rib cage with knotted towels."

    —PETER ANDREWS, writer

"You can, legally, possibly hit and kill a fellow golfer with a ball, and there will not be a lot of trouble because the other golfers will refuse to stop and be witnesses because they will want to keep playing."

    —DAVE BARRY, humorist

FUTILITY

"It took me 17 years to get 3,000 hits in baseball. I did it in one afternoon on the golf course."

    —HANK AARON, Hall of Famer

GALLERY

"Watching a golf tournament is different from attending other sporting events. For one thing, the drunks are spread out in a larger area."

    —DON WADE, writer

"One of life's great mysteries is just what do golfers think they are playing at. But even more mysterious is what those spectators who traipse around golf courses are looking for."

    —MICHAEL PARKINSON, president of the Anti-Golf Society

"There is one thing in this world that is dumber than playing golf. That is watching someone else play golf. What do you actually get to see? Thirty-seven guys in polyester slacks squinting in the sun. Doesn't that set your blood racing?"

    —PETER ANDREWS, writer

GIMME

"Gimme: an agreement between two losers who can't putt."
>—JIM BISHOP, syndicated columnist

GOD

"So, it's me again, huh, Lord? Why don't you just come down here and we'll play. And bring that kid of yours. I'll play your best ball."
>—TOMMY BOLT, after blowing another putt

"Golf is the Lord's punishment for man's sins."
>—JAMES "SCOTTY" RESTON, *New York Times* columnist

GOLF

"In golf, when we hit a foul ball, we got to go out and play it."
  —SAM SNEAD to baseball legend Ted Williams

"Golf is not a funeral, though both can be very sad affairs."
  —BERNARD DARWIN, English golfer and writer

"Golf does strange things to people. It makes liars out of honest men, cheats out of altruists, cowards out of brave men, and fools out of everybody."
  —MILTON GROSS, author

"According to locker room lore, the name golf arose by default—all the other four-letter words had already been taken."
  —GEORGE PEPER, writer

"Golf is a game in which you yell 'fore,' shoot six, and write down five."
  —PAUL HARVEY, news commentator

"Golf is just a game—and an idiotic game most of the time."
　　—MARK CALCAVECCHIA, PGA pro

"Golf is a funny game, but it wasn't meant to be."
　　—CHARLES PRICE, writer

"Golf giveth and golf taketh away, but it taketh away a hell of a lot more than it giveth."
　　—SIMON HOBDAY, Senior PGA pro

"If you watch a game, it's fun. If you play it, it's recreation. If you work at it, it's golf."
　　—BOB HOPE

GOLF AND FOOTBALL

"In football . . . some coaches have stated, 'When you throw a pass, three things can happen, two of them are bad.' In golf, there is no limit."
—MARINO PARASCENZO, sportswriter

"Golf lacks something for me. It would be better if once in a while someone came up from behind and tackled you just as you were hitting the ball."
—RED GRANGE, football legend

GOLF AND SEX

"Golf and masturbation have at least one thing in common: Both are a lot more satisfying to do than they are to watch."
—Anonymous

"Golf and sex are about the only things you can enjoy without being good at it."
　　—JIMMY DEMARET

GOLF CRITICS

"Golf seems to me an arduous way to go for a walk. I prefer to take the dogs out."
　　—PRINCESS ANNE

"Golf is a game whose aim is to hit a very small ball into a very small hole, with weapons singularly ill-designed for the purpose."
　　—WINSTON CHURCHILL

"Golf is a good walk spoiled."
　　—MARK TWAIN

"If you want to take long walks, take long walks. If you want to hit things with a stick, hit things with a stick. But there's no excuse for combining the two and putting the results on TV. Golf is not so much a sport as an assault to lawns."
    —National Lampoon

"Golf is the most useless outdoor game ever devised to waste time and try the spirit of man."
    —WESTBROOK PEGLER, sportswriter

"Golf is a game of such monumental stupidity that anyone with a brain more active than a cantaloupe has difficulty gearing down to its demands."
    —PETER ANDREWS, writer

"All I've got against golf is it takes you so far from the clubhouse."
    —ERIC LINKLATER, Scottish novelist

"Many play golf, and one odd effect of that pursuit is that they return to work manifestly stupider than they were. It is, I think, the company of other golfers."

—G.W. LYTTLETON, British public official

"The reason I don't play golf is because I was a caddie when I was 13. Women never gave up a ball that was lost somewhere in the trees and thicket and down through the poison ivy. It was during one of these searches that I vowed to the Lord above that if I ever earned enough money I would never set foot on a course again."

—ART BUCHWALD, humorist

"There are now more golf clubs in the world than Gideon bibles, more golf balls than missionaries, and, if every golfer in the world, male and female, were laid end to end, I, for one, would leave them there."

—MICHAEL PARKINSON, president of the Anti-Golf Society

GOLF GAME

"Yes, a lot more people beat me now."

> —DWIGHT D. EISENHOWER, when asked if his game had changed since leaving the White House

"My game is so bad I gotta hire three caddies—one to walk the left rough, one for the right rough, and one down the middle. And the one in the middle doesn't have much to do."

> —DAVE HILL, Senior PGA pro

GOLF SWING

"My God, he looks like he's beating a chicken."

> —BYRON NELSON, analyzing actor Jack Lemmon's swing

"Gay Brewer swings the club in a figure eight. If you didn't know better, you'd swear he was trying to kill snakes."

> —DAVE HILL, fellow Senior PGA pro

"The pivot is the utilization of multiple centers to produce a circular motion for generating centrifugal force on an adjusted plane, plus the maintenance of balance necessary to promote the two-line delivery path."

 —J.C. ANDERSEN, PGA pro, on his tongue-in-cheek secret
  to the perfect golf swing

"Dividing the swing into its parts is like dissecting a cat. You'll have blood and guts and bones all over the place. But you won't have a cat."

 —ERNEST JONES, who taught golf for more than half a century

"The golfer who stands at the ball as rigid as a statue usually becomes a monumental failure."

 —DICK AULTMAN, golf instructor

"When you look up and cause an awful shot, you will always look down again at exactly the moment you ought to start watching the ball if you ever want to see it again."
—HENRY BEARD, author

"The golf swing is among the most stressful and unnatural acts in sports, short of cheering for the Yankees."
—BRAD FAXON, PGA pro

"When I learned to play golf, I had to run from the groundskeeper. He was always taking shots at me, and I had to swing fast."
—CHI CHI RODRIGUEZ, on why he's a speedy player

GOOD LOSER

"Show me a good loser and I'll show you a seldom winner."

    —SAM SNEAD

GREENS

"If I'm breathing heavy while walking on a green, I'm going uphill. If I trip, I'm going downhill."

    —SPEC GOLDMAN, elderly golfer, on how he reads the greens

"The greens are harder than a whore's heart."

    —SAM SNEAD, on the greens at Winged Foot Golf Club

GRIP

"I think I'll change my grip."

    —BILL THOMAS, amateur, after his slice broke the windshields of two passing vehicles

"I've been squeezing the club so hard the cow is screaming."
  —J.C. SNEAD

"If a lot of people gripped a knife and fork the way they do a golf club, they'd starve to death."
  —SAM SNEAD

HANDICAPS

"My handicap? Woods and irons."
  —CHRIS CODIROLI, former major league pitcher

"I can't give you a number, but I'm down to one arm."
  —DAVE DRAVECKY, former big league pitcher, now an amputee, when asked his handicap at a pro-am

"Nothing goes down slower than a golf handicap."
  —BOBBY NICHOLS, golf pro

HOLE IN ONE

*"There are two reasons for making a hole in one.
The first is that it is immensely laborsaving."*
—H.I. PHILLIPS, writer

"I find it to be the hole in one."
—GROUCHO MARX, when asked about the most difficult shot

"It was a hole in one contest and I had a three."
—ABE LEMONS, Texas basketball coach, explaining how he came
within two strokes of winning an automobile in a golf tournament

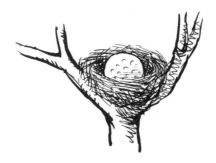

HUSBANDS AND WIVES

"Golf is undertaken mostly by husbands and wives over nine holes on Friday evenings or Sunday afternoons, when nothing better is scheduled, often with results so discordant they make Ralph and Alice Kramden sound positively blissful by contrast."

  —NICK SEITZ, writer, on foursome play in golf

"Golf is played by 20 million mature American men whose wives think they are out there having fun."

  —JIM BISHOP, columnist

"Playing with your spouse on the golf course runs almost as great a marital risk as getting caught playing with someone else's anywhere else."

  —PETER ANDREWS, writer

"Many men are more faithful to their golf partners than to their wives and have stuck with them longer."

  —JOHN UPDIKE, author

INSANITY

"Have you ever actually listened to golfers talking to each other? 'Looked good starting out.' . . . 'Better direction than last time.' . . . 'Who's away?' It sounds like a visitor's day at a home for the criminally insane."
—PETER ANDREWS, writer

"As every golfer knows, no one ever lost his mind over one shot. It is rather the gradual process of shot after shot watching your score go to tatters . . . knowing that you have found a different way to bogey each one."
—THOMAS BOSWELL, sportswriter

"One hundred years of experience has demonstrated that the game is temporary insanity practiced in a pasture."
—DAVE KINDRED, sportswriter

INSTRUCTION

"The reason the pro tells you to keep your head down is so you can't see him laughing."
—PHYLLIS DILLER, comedienne

"First, hitting the ball. Second, finding out where it went."
—TOM WATSON, explaining the two most important lessons for helping a bad golfer with his game

"Then came the more foreboding realization that my trying to teach him rhythm and pace might be like Archie Bunker helping William Shakespeare write drama."
—DICK AULTMAN, golf instructor, on teaching a gifted student

"Air mail without zip code will never find its target."
—BOB TOSKI, golf instructor, on trading distance for accuracy

"Frank, either you have to get better soon or quit telling people I'm your teacher."

—DAVE MARR to NFL Hall of Famer Frank Gifford, on his golf game

IQ

"I owe everything to golf. Where else could a guy with an IQ like mine make this much money?"

—HUBERT GREEN

"My IQ must be two points lower than a plant's."

—TOM WATSON, after being disqualified for changing putters in the middle of a rain-suspended round of the 1986 Vantage Championship

LIFE EXPECTANCY

"Every round I play, I shorten my life by two years."
    —TOMMY NAKAJIMA, golf pro

LUCK

"My luck is so bad that if I bought a cemetery, people would stop dying."
    —ED FURGOL, Senior PGA pro

MENTAL GAME

"The worst club in my bag is my brain."
    —CHRIS PERRY, PGA pro

"I've injured both my hands playing golf and they're okay now, but my brain has always been somewhat suspect."
　　—BOB MURPHY, pro golfer

"Thinking must be the hardest thing to do in golf, because we do so little of it."
　　—HARVEY PENICK, noted golf instructor

MISHAP

"He was standing too close to my ball."
　　—BARRY GOLDWATER, after beaning a spectator 30 yards
　　　off the tee at the Phoenix Open Pro-Am, 1965

"I know I'm getting better at golf because I'm hitting fewer spectators."
　　—GERALD R. FORD

MULLIGAN

"Mulligan: invented by an Irishman who wanted to hit one more 20-yard grounder."
> —JIM BISHOP, columnist

"It's often necessary to hit a second shot to really appreciate the first one."
> —HENRY BEARD, author

NERVES

"You know what I did here one year? I was so nervous I drank a fifth of rum before I played. I shot the happiest 83 of my life."
> —CHI CHI RODRIGUEZ

"I am so tense at times that I can hear the bees farting."
> —MICK O'LOUGHLIN, Irish pro, in 1938

"Class, someone once said, is the ability to undergo pressure with grace. So what did I do? I just did what comes naturally.
I vomited."

    —CHARLES PRICE, writer, on leading a club tournament

"Some guys get so nervous playing for their own money, the greens don't need fertilizing for a year."

    —DAVE HILL, pro golfer

"I would rather open on Broadway in Hamlet, with no rehearsals, than tee off at Pebble Beach in the tournament."

    —JACK LEMMON, actor, on playing the Bing Crosby
       National Pro-Am

"My butterflies are still going strong. I just hope they are flying in formation."

    —LARRY MIZE, on playing with a big lead

19TH HOLE

"If I try to leave the hotel tonight, put out a contract on me."
> —DAVE MARR, PGA pro, after starting a round with a hangover

"The way I hit the ball today, I need to go to the range. Instead, I think I'll go to the bar."
> —FUZZY ZOELLER, at the 1984 PGA Championship

"I like to say I was born on the 19th hole—the only one I ever parred."
> —GEORGE LOW, touring pro

OPTIMIST

"I try to put myself in a great frame of mind before I go out— then I screw it up with the first shot."
> —JOHNNY MILLER

"Chip Beck [1993 Masters runner-up] is such a positive, upbeat person, if a car ran over and killed his dog, he'd marvel at how peaceful the poor beast looked."
—GARY McCORD, TV analyst and part-time pro

PATIENCE

"I told Mac O'Grady that he had to learn patience. Damned if he doesn't go to Palm Springs and do nothing but drive behind elderly people for the entire day. I don't know if that taught him patience, but it almost got him arrested twice."
—GARY McCORD, TV analyst and part-time pro

PEBBLE BEACH

"Pebble Beach and Cypress Point make you want to play golf, they're such interesting and enjoyable layouts. Spyglass Hill, now that's different; that makes you want to go fishing."

    —JACK NICKLAUS

"It's a 300-acre unplayable lie."

    —JIM MURRAY, sportswriter

"I've heard of unplayable lies, but on the tee?"

    —BOB HOPE

PINE VALLEY

"Pine Valley is the shrine of American golf because so many golfers are buried there."

    —ED SULLIVAN, American television personality

POOR PLAY

"No self-respecting pro should ever shoot 86."

—GRIER JONES, PGA pro, the day before he shot an 85

"I played so bad, I got a get-well card from the IRS."

—JOHNNY MILLER, on his terrible 1977 season

"Easy. I missed a 20-footer for a 12."

—ARNOLD PALMER, at the 1961 Los Angeles Open, when asked how he managed to make a 13 on one hole

"I'm playing like Tarzan—and scoring like Jane."

—CHI CHI RODRIGUEZ, at the 1970 Masters

"All my life I wanted to play like Jack Nicklaus, and now I do."

—PAUL HARVEY, news commentator, after Nicklaus shot an 83 at the 1981 British Open

"Please forward this check to charity to help the cost of all the condo windows I broke during my play here."

> —GARY McCORD, after he won $2,000 in the Bob Hope Chrysler Classic

"Give me a banana. I'm playing like a monkey, why not eat like one?"

> —CHI CHI RODRIGUEZ

"I was afraid to move my lips in front of the TV cameras. The commissioner probably would have fined me just for what I was thinking."

> —TOM WEISKOPF, on his 13 on the 12th hole in the 1980 Masters

"I started my career off very slow—then I tapered off."

> —GARY McCORD, TV analyst and part-time PGA pro

POTENTIAL

"I told him he was a year away from the Tour and next year he'll be two years away."
> —CHI CHI RODRIGUEZ, when asked to evaluate an amateur's potential

PRAYER

"Prayer never seems to work for me on the golf course. I think this has something to do with my being a terrible putter."
> —The REVEREND BILLY GRAHAM

"I never pray on the golf course. Actually, the Lord answers my prayers everywhere except on the course."
> —The REVEREND BILLY GRAHAM

PROFANITY

"Golf is a game of expletives not deleted."
—Dr. IRVING A. GLADSTONE, author

"If profanity had any influence on the flight of the ball, the game would be played far better than it is."
—HORACE G. HUTCHINSON, golf historian

PUTTERS

"Drown, you poor bastard, drown!"
—KY LAFFOON, while grabbing his putter by the neck of the shaft and shoving it underwater after blowing a putt

"That's a bagful of indecisions."
—JACK BURKE, 1956 PGA champion, on Arnold Palmer's eight putters

"If I had to choose between my wife and my putter, well, I'd miss her."
> —GARY PLAYER, on the putter he's used since 1967

"I call my putter 'Sweet Charity' because it covers such a multitude of sins from tee to green."
> —BILLY CASPER, Senior PGA pro

"Why am I using a new putter? Because the old one didn't float too well."
> —CRAIG STADLER, at the 1993 U.S. Open

"My caddie had the best answer for why I carry two putters: 'Just to let the other one know it can be replaced.'"
> —LARRY NELSON, PGA pro

PUTTING

*"I had some uphill putts—after each of my
downhill putts."*
> —HOMERO BLANCAS, after shooting a 77 at the 1974 U.S. Open

*"Few pleasures on earth match the feeling that comes
from making a loud bodily-function noise just as a guy is
about to putt."*
> —DAVE BARRY, humorist

**"The devoted golfer is an anguished soul who has
learned a lot about putting just as an avalanche victim
has learned a lot about snow."**
> —DAN JENKINS, author

"Ninety percent of putts that are short don't go in."
> —YOGI BERRA, baseball Hall of Famer and observer of life

**"Not only are three-putt greens probable, at times they're
an achievement."**
> —CHARLEY PRIDE, country singer

"I never lost a ball today, but my putting let me down. I lost my putting in Mexico City . . . in 1953."

> —ALBERT PELISSIER, the plucky Frenchman who, at age 68, shot a 28-over-par 97 at the 1986 Monte Carlo Open

QUITTING

"When they start hitting back at you, it's time to quit."

> —HENRY RANSOM, PGA pro, after a shot ricocheted off a rocky Cypress Point cliff and hit him

"Golf is a game that everybody quits, but nobody stops playing."

> —BILL DAVIS, founder, *Golf Digest*

REMEMBERING SHOTS

"I find it to be more satisfying to be a bad player at golf. The worse you play, the better you remember the occasional good shot."
> —NUBAR GULBENKIAN, Middle East financier

"Strokes always accumulate faster than they can be forgotten."
> —HENRY BEARD, author

Some golfers lie awake at night
And brood on what went wrong;
I'd rather think of what went right.
It doesn't take as long.
> —DICK EMMONS, golf fan

"Let a pro hit 999 of 1,000 shots perfect and he curses the golfing gods because of the one unfortunate shot. Let an amateur hit 999 of 1,000 shots poorly but hit one perfectly and he exalts the game."
> —MAC O'GRADY, PGA pro

RETIREMENT

"My ultimate desire is to retire from the game because it drives me berserk."

—DAVID FEHERTY, Irish pro

"I retired from competition at 28, the same age as Bobby Jones. The difference was that Jones retired because he beat everybody. I retired because I couldn't beat anybody."

—CHARLES PRICE, author

RULES

"You cannot ground your club in addressing the ball, or move anything, however loose or dead it may be."

—Royal Selanger Golf Club, built on an ancient Chinese burial ground near Kuala Lampur

"Golf, in fact, is the only game in the world in which a precise knowledge of the rules can earn one a reputation for bad sportsmanship."
>   —PATRICK CAMPBELL, golf instructor

ST. ANDREWS

"There's nothing wrong with the St. Andrews course that one hundred bulldozers couldn't put right. The Old Course needs a dry-clean and press."
>   —ED FURGOL, Senior PGA pro

"The Old Course is an uninteresting stretch of drab linksland. It has so many bunkers that I get the feeling somebody goes out in the dark to dig new ones."
>   —FRED DALY, 1947 British Open champion

SCOREKEEPING

"When you catch your ass in a buzz saw, it's not too easy to tell how many teeth bit you."
> —Scorer to pro Brian Barnes, who had just 12-putted the 8th hole at the 1968 French Open

"Only in America can I sign a wrong card and become a national hero. In my country, they would run me out of town for doing such a stupid thing."
> —Argentine-born ROBERTO DeVICENZO, after losing the 1968 Masters because he mistakenly signed an incorrect scorecard

SENIORS

"Old golfers never die. They just lose their balls."
> —bumper sticker

"I didn't realize how long some of these seniors have been around. Yesterday I saw a guy signing his scorecard with a feather."
—BOB HOPE

"Golf became increasingly harder for me. I shot in the 60s in the 1960s, the 70s in the 1970s, and the 80s in the 1980s."
—PHIL RODGERS, Senior PGA pro

"You know you're on the Senior Tour when your back goes out more often than you do."
—BOB BRUE, Senior PGA pro

"Old golfers don't fade away. We just lose our distance."
—RALPH GUDAHL, former PGA pro

"Some of these legends have been around golf a long time. When they mention a good grip, they're talking about their dentures."
—BOB HOPE

"The older you get, the longer you used to be."
 —CHI CHI RODRIGUEZ

"In 30 years we're going to be in our 90s. We're going to play three-hole tournaments for $900,000, and the one who remembers his score wins."
 —BOB BRUE, Senior PGA pro

"Like a lot of fellows on the Senior Tour, I have a furniture problem. My chest has fallen into my drawers."
 —BILLY CASPER, Senior PGA pro

"No matter how bad you get, you can probably still make money playing the Senile Old Golfers Pro Tour."
 —DAVE BARRY, humorist

"When you get up there in years, the fairways get longer and the holes get smaller."
 —BOBBY LOCKE, South African pro

SLICE

The golfer finds that turkey day
Is not all that enticing.
Although I've put my clubs away,
It's one more chance for slicing.
> —DICK EMMONS, golf fan

"I quit playing."
> —PHIL HARRIS, comedian, on how he cured his chronic slice

"That's what we call a Lorena Bobbitt. A nasty slice."
> —GARY McCORD, TV analyst and part-time pro, describing
> a shot at the 1994 Phoenix Open

"I'm not saying my golf game went bad, but if I grew tomatoes, they'd come up sliced."
> —LEE TREVINO

SLOW PLAY

"You start your soft-boiled eggs by the time he's ready."
> —JOHNNY MILLER, on the slow play of 1990 Masters winner
> Nick Faldo

***"Don't blame me for being late. Blame the foursome
ahead of me."***
> —All-Pro linebacker LAWRENCE TAYLOR, upon arriving late for
> the New York Giants training camp

*"There was a thunderous crack like cannon fire and suddenly
I was lifted a foot and a half off the ground. . . . Damn,
I thought to myself, this is a helluva penalty for slow play."*
> —LEE TREVINO, on being struck by lightning

***"Are you waiting for inspiration or have you suddenly
taken ill?"***
> —"PADDY" HANMER, past club secretary at Muirfield, shouting
> at a slow club member

"If the following foursome is pressing you, wave them through—and then speed up."

    —DEANE BEMAN, PGA Tour commissioner

SPORTSMANSHIP

"It's good sportsmanship to not pick up lost balls while they are still rolling."

    —MARK TWAIN

SPORTS PSYCHOLOGISTS

"I've gone to a half dozen sports psychologists. Each time, he gave me my money back and told me to go to another guy and drive him crazy."

    —J.C. ANDERSEN, PGA pro

SUFFERING

"Golf has taught me there is a connection between pain and pleasure. Golf spelled backwards is flog."
> —PHYLLIS DILLER, comedienne

"Golf is the cruelest of sports and like life, it's unfair. It's a harlot. A trollop. It leads you on. It never lives up to promises. It's not a sport, it's bondage. An obsession. A boulevard of broken dreams. It plays with men. And runs off with the butcher."
> —JIM MURRAY, sportswriter

"I've just heard that soon he might be well enough to play golf. Hasn't the man suffered enough?"
> —PAUL HARVEY, radio commentator, on an artificial-heart transplant recipient

TEE TIME

"Hell, I don't even get up at that hour to close the window."

—WALTER HAGEN, ignoring an early tee time

TELEVISION

"I don't like to watch golf on television. I can't stand whispering."

—DAVID BRENNER, comedian

"Anyone who likes golf on television would enjoy watching the grass grow on the greens."

—ANDY ROONEY, columnist and TV commentator

TEMPER

"I buried a few [clubs], you know. It took two men to get one of them out."

—DAVE HILL, pro golfer

"Mr. Byers and I played terribly. He was a veteran and I was a youngster, but we expressed our feelings in exactly the same way. When we missed a shot, we threw the club away. I think the main reason I beat him was because he ran out of clubs first."
    —BOBBY JONES

"Golf is a game that creates emotions that sometimes cannot be sustained with the club still in one's hand."
    —BOBBY JONES

"Golf always makes me so damned angry."
    —KING GEORGE V

"I broke my toe once by taking an enormous kick at my bag. It was very satisfying—until the point of contact."
    —DAVID FEHERTY, Irish pro

"Always throw clubs ahead of you. That way, you don't have to waste energy going back to pick them up."
    —TOMMY "THUNDER" BOLT

"I can't believe the actions of some of our top pros. They should have side jobs modeling for Pampers."
    —FUZZY ZOELLER

TOUGH SHOTS

"To illustrate how difficult this shot is, go out into your front yard and chip a ball from your lawn down onto the hood of your car and make it stop. Pretty hard to do, huh? Well, this is tougher."
    —GARY McCORD to TV viewers, on an approach to the 16th hole at the Memorial

"The hardest shot is the chip at 90 yards from the green where the ball has to be played against an oak tree, bounces back into a sandtrap, hits a stone, bounces onto the green, and then rolls into the cup. That shot is so difficult, I have only made it once."
 —ZEPPO MARX, comic actor

ULCERS

"Golf is neither a microcosm of nor a metaphor for life. It is a sport, a bloodless sport, if you don't count ulcers."
 —DICK SCHAAP, author

"Golf is a game where guts, stick-to-it-iveness, and blind devotion will get you nothing but an ulcer."
 —TOMMY BOLT

U.S. OPEN

"Playing in the U.S. Open is like tippy-toeing through hell."
—JERRY McGEE, PGA pro

"If you like driving in Memorial Day weekend traffic and going to movies like Glory where everybody gets killed at the end, you'll love the Open. It isn't a golf tournament, it's a survival test."
—NICK SEITZ, writer

VIDEO GOLF

"I don't enjoy playing video golf because there's nothing to throw."
—PAUL AZINGER

WAR

"It's nice to see a president improving his golf game with the nation on the brink of war. On the eve of Fort Sumter, they say Lincoln was so nervous he was blowing routine six-foot putts."

> —GERALD NACHMAN, columnist, about President George Bush playing golf after Iraq invaded Kuwait

WATER HAZARDS

"Two balls in the water. By God, I've got a good mind to jump in and make it four!"

> —SIMON HOBDAY, after plunking two shots into the drink at the 1994 Senior PGA Championship

"I've lost balls in every hazard and on every course I've tried. But when I lose a ball in the ball washer it's time to take stock."

> —MILTON GROSS, author

"Water creates a neurosis in golfers. The very thought of this harmless fluid robs them of their normal powers of rational thought, turns their legs to jelly, and produces a palsy of the upper limbs."

—PETER DOBEREINER, writer

"I kind of wished I had some scuba diving equipment so I could retrieve all the balls we hit into the water. I probably would have made more money than I did for winning the thing."

—LEE TREVINO, on the 1994 Seniors Championship

WEATHER

"The wind was so strong there were whitecaps in the porta-john."

—JOYCE KAZMIERSKI, LPGA pro, commenting on the weather conditions at the 1983 Women's Kemper Open

"I'm sure glad we don't have to play in the shade."
>—WALTER HAGEN, when told at a match in Florida that
>   it was 105 degrees in the shade

*"I play in the low 80s. If it's any hotter than that,
I won't play."*
>—JOE E. LEWIS, comedian

WOODS

**"Ben Crenshaw hits in the woods so often he should
get an orange hunting jacket."**
>—TOM WEISKOPF

*"I'm hitting the woods great, but I'm having trouble getting
out of them."*
>—HARRY TOSCANO, Senior PGA pro

"I only see Charley Pride when we get to the greens. Charley hits some good wood—most of them are trees."
    —GLEN CAMPBELL, singer

WORK

"Golf kept me from taking an honest job. My theory is never work for a living if you don't have to."
    —DON JANUARY, Senior PGA pro

WRONG BALL

"If you think it's hard to meet new people, try picking up the wrong ball."
    —JACK LEMMON, actor

YOUTH

"I was so skinny when I was a kid that I got my start in golf as a ball marker."
        —CHI CHI RODRIGUEZ

"The game was easy for me as a kid, and I had to play a while to find out how hard it is."
        —RAYMOND FLOYD, after winning the 1976 Masters